thoughtless

Yasmine Shehata

BookLeaf Publishing

India | USA | UK

Presentation by *BookLeaf Publishing*

Web: www.bookleafpub.com

E-mail: info@bookleafpub.com

ISBN: 9789358316872

First edition 2024

Submerged

Maybe we grew up too fast.
Thrown into the deep,
Not even told to swim.
"Just don't drown".
And even on our last limb,
We'd stay quiet,
We'd push through,
We'd fight to survive.
Yet, you didn't seem to care.
Then you wondered why-
--Why we became bitter.
Because only we knew.
When life happens too soon,
We grow up even faster.

Fraud

In the shadows deep, I wear a mask.
A fraud, a charlatan, a daunting task.
I smile and play the part so well, yet deep
within, my secrets dwell.
I dance upon a fragile thread. Where truth and
falsehood interbred. I was a clock of the lies so
thin, afraid the world would see within.
But in the night, I face my fears.
The mirrors' truth, my bitter tears. For in this
game of make-believe, my soul, myself I cannot
decide.
I yearn to shed this fraud's disguise. To face the
world with honest eyes.
To be the me I long to be.
And from the fraud, and at least be free.

Finite

To cease to exist,
In space.
In time.
To perish.
Simply, disappear.
And in a moment where time stands still,
a moment of irrelevance
Everything finally stands still.
Only a memory lives on.
And in that moment,
to cease to exist
Is like falling into an eternal sleep.

Unspoken words

We vowed silence.
But what happened when
Our silence was too heavy
and waged war
We are left with nothing
But our words.

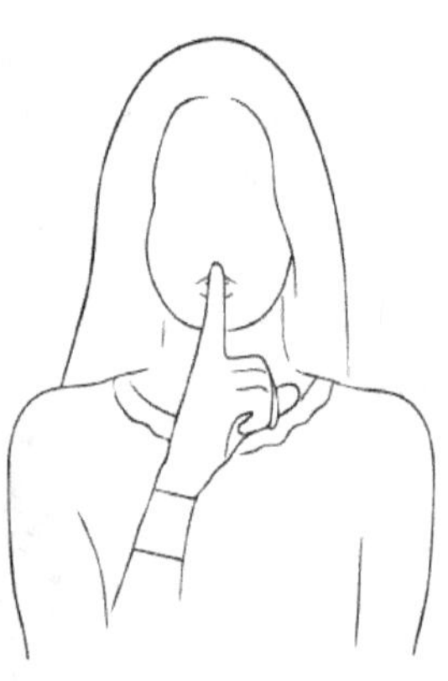

Olive Branch

From the river to the sea,
For every shiver and plea,
There will be justice and peace.
Our people will no longer flee,
And our heartbeats will never retreat,
A story of sadness and courage,
We will never be discouraged.
For one day,
Palestine will be free.

One too many

Just one more day.
To kiss the pain away,
Just one more day,
For a hug that was my drug.
Just one more day,
So our smile could last a little while.
And everything felt worthwhile.
If only we had
Just one more day.

What is home?

Where I love is home.
Where the salty air touches my lips
and
The sun dances on my skin.
Where the chaotic beauty of life
Fills the air.
And in the chaotic uncertainty
That is where I find my peace.
Then it occurs to me,
that is home.

Living

Dear life,
We always knew things wouldn't last forever. So we enjoyed having you around for what felt like forever.

And suddenly, things changed. In a race against the last sand grain, everything became indefinite. Nothing lasts forever, yet anything but this eternity was too unimagine.

Nostalgic

I miss the old days.
Before we grew up.
Where our real worries weren't real,
and our laughter was unattainable -
yet now unimaginable.
Our tears were but a bluff
And time was never enough.
Take me back to a time,
Where depression didn't exist
And anxiety wasn't even butterflies.
Take me back in time.
The last time I was truly happy.

Gone

Your laughter, a melody, my heart's delight,
A symphony of days and endless nights,
In your embrace, I found my home,
A love so deep, I thought it would never roam.

But seasons change, and love can fade,
The echoes of your presence slowly wane,
Yet in the quiet of memories, there remains,
A love that once bloomed, that still sustains.

Though your love may be a chapter past,
Its impression on my soul forever cast,
I'll treasure the moments we were once beloved,
For love, once given, can never truly be
removed.

Adoration

In your presence, my heart takes flight,
A symphony of emotions, pure and bright.
With every glance and every smile,
I'm lost in your charm for a while.

Your eyes, like stars, in the midnight sky,
Hold secrets and wonders I can't deny.
A gentle touch, a voice so sweet,
In your adoration,
I find my heartbeat.

Soft lies

Hidden in the corner of watchful eyes,
They wore a cloak of innocence and disguise,
a tender falsehood, like peaceful grey skies.

Though easy on the ear soft lies
Fester and grow, bringing forth fear,
A facade of comfort, a gentle guise,
Beneath it all, is a truth that belies.

And as honesty remains the key,
For soft lies, however gentle they be,
Cannot replace the light of the truth,
In the search for honesty, we find our youth.

Eternal Revolve

In the dance of time, round and round,
Where beginnings and ends are seldom found,
Circles of life, of love, of day and night,
Revolving in endless loops, pure and bright.

Spinning tales of destiny, fate's device,
Every revolution, a roll of the dice,
Yet in each turn, in the rhythm we solve,
The universe's mystery, as we revolve.

Inadequate Whisphers

In shadows cast by doubt's cold hand,
I've heard inadequacy's whispering stand.
Yet within our flaws, we find our grace,
A journey through darkness to a brighter place.

Embrace imperfection, for in that divide,
We discover the strength to grow, to ride
The waves of self-doubt, into the unknown,
Where inadequacy's hushed voice is overthrown.

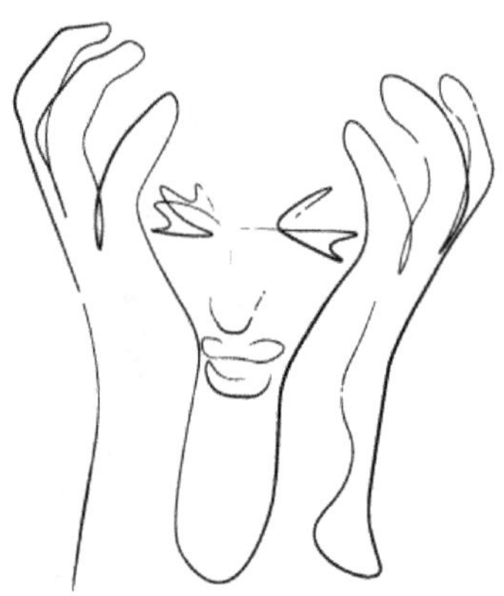

Discovering Inner Peace

Amid life's tempests and the constant noise,
In solitude's embrace, the heart finds balance.
Seeking serenity in the depths within,
A tranquil journey where we all begin.

With each mindful breath, a step we take,
Toward inner peace, a soothing, gentle lake.
Calm waters mirror the soul's release,
In stillness and presence, we find our inner
peace.

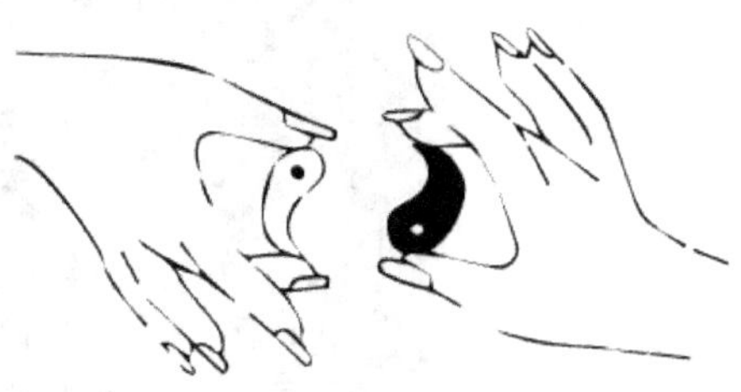

Depths of Hopelessness

In the depths of despair, when all seems lost,
Hopelessness blankets the soul, a heavy cost.
But even in darkness, a spark may reside,
A glimmer of hope, a reason to abide.

When the world's weight bears down on your chest,
Remember, my friend, hope's not laid to rest.
Though the road is steep and filled with despair,
A sliver of light may yet linger there.

Broken Hearts

You broke me.
All the love,
The hours,
The memories spent with you -
Suddenly no longer existed.
And I was supposed to be "Just fine".
But as that last message,
as I clicked send
tore my heart into a million parts.

Timeless

Through seasons of change and years that pass,
Our friendship endures, like polished glass.
A bond so strong, it can weather all,
In the face of time, it will never fall.

With laughter and tears, we've journeyed along,
In the chorus of life, you are my song.
A timeless friendship, an unbroken line,
In the tapestry of our lives, forever intertwined.

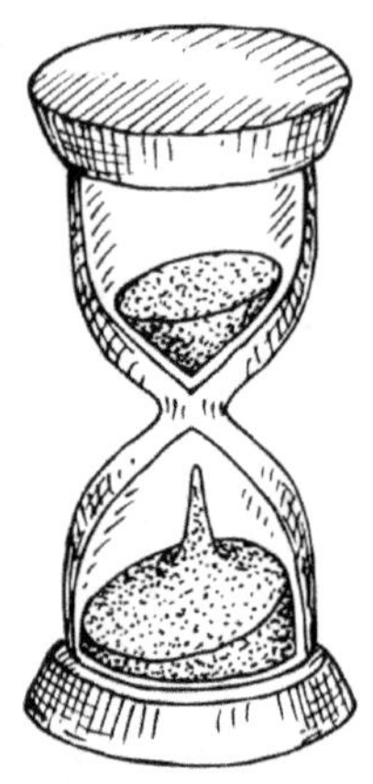

Fascinatingly Normal

In the everyday moments, we often find,
A magic hidden, to most, undefined.
A mundane world, with beauty concealed,
In ordinary acts, true wonders revealed.

A smile exchanged on a crowded street,
Or raindrops on leaves, a rhythm so sweet.
Romancing the mundane, we redefine,
The ordinary as special, in every line.

A simple meal shared, a table for a few,
In these simple moments, love can renew.
In life's little details, so plain and pure,
We find the extraordinary, that's for sure.

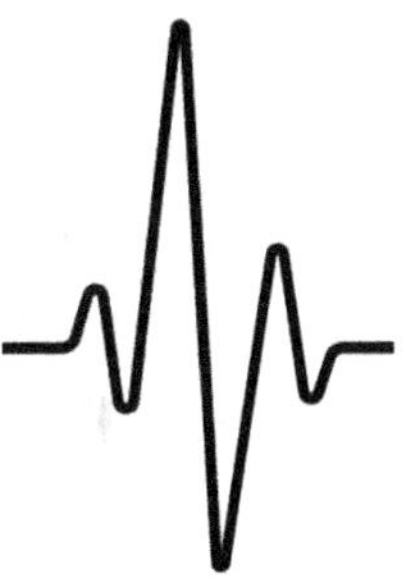

Fear

In shadows deep, where fears reside,
In the heart's chamber, where doubts collide,
The trembling soul, in the dark of night,
Grapples with terrors, shrouded in fright.

Yet within that fear, a courage stirs,
A force to confront what life confers.
For in facing the unknown, we find our might,
And transform the darkness into guiding light

Delirium's Dance

In the fevered haze of a restless mind,
Delirium takes its curious bind.
Thoughts a whirlwind, a chaotic trance,
In the realm of dreams, we find our chance.

Reality blurs and senses wane,
As delirium's grip pulls at the rein.
In this disarray, where worlds collide,
We glimpse the depths where secrets hide.

Through the kaleidoscope of a fevered dream,
Delirium's dance, a wild, untamed stream.
In the agony of madness, we may roam,
Yet in this chaos, we find our own home.